Mysteries, True and False

Story by **Hubert Ben Kemoun**
Factual accounts by **François Aulas**
Activities by **Béatrice Garel** and **François Aulas**
Game by **Catherine Pauwels**

Contents

True	This is a verified story or, perhaps, a legend. In any case, there is a mystery that science has been unable to explain.
False	The mystery has been revealed. Science has provided the explanation.

Quiz

Stickers

Picture Cards

Old Solem

Hubert Ben Kemoun

Remember Your Magic!

Bullit, the richest farmer on the
island, placed himself squarely in
front of Old Solem, sweat running
down his face. The little electric fan
barely stirred the air in the room.

"You were a great sorcerer,
Solem—the greatest that our island
has ever known."

"That was long ago," replied the
old man. He was seated in his armchair, his attention not on his visitor,
but on the TV.

"Solem, it has not rained for
three months. It is a disaster! You
must do something! You, the old
sorcerer of the Motecks, can make it
rain!" said the farmer.

Solem snorted. "You dare speak of the Motecks! There are no more than thirty of us left. You have stolen our land. What more do you want from us? Now go and leave me alone. I will lose track of my program."

"I will pay you well if you can make it rain."

Solem's hands trembled on the arms of his chair. Some people on the island of Yatag claimed that he was not right in the head, that too many years and not enough money had changed the old man. But most felt that the most powerful of the sorcerers couldn't have lost his gift.

"I will pay you in dollars—many dollars," said Bullit.

Solem looked up, his eyes sad. "Once I knew the secret signs, the mysterious keys that opened the gates of the heavens. But I long ago lost my magic."

"Find it again! I will make you a rich man!"

"Rich?"

"Yes, very rich. But you must make it rain."

"So what are you saying? You can make my fortune, but you cannot make it rain?" Solem asked.

Bullit ignored the contempt in Solem's voice. "You will try?" he asked.

There was a long silence. "Yes, I will try," said the old man finally.

"And you will succeed! By this very night! My fields are dry! My animals need water!"

"By tonight . . ." muttered the old man.

"Good! You will not be sorry," Bullit shouted as went out the door. "Remember—make it rain and I'll make you rich!"

The First Spell

It is said on the island of Yatag that Old Solem did not sleep that night. People claimed they saw him put on the old headdress of the Moteck sorcerers and heard him invoke the heavens, his trembling hands raised toward the stars.

"Was it you that did it?" shouted Bullit, bursting into Solem's parlor. He was beside himself. He pointed out the window. He wiped the perspiration that ran down his neck and waited for an explanation.

"It is possible. I told you yesterday that I had forgotten the ancient spells," the old man said, without taking his eyes from the flickering TV.

Since the middle of the morning, a thick fog had spread over Yatag. Dense and dark, it clung to the trees and swirled around the houses, making the air even more stifling than before.

"You will try again tonight!" ordered Bullit, a cold smile on his red face. "This time you will succeed. You *must* succeed. Your house is on my land. Do not forget that I can throw you out at any time."

"Is that a threat?" asked Old Solem.

"It's not a threat, it's a deal. I'm a businessman. This land is mine."

"And now you want tears from heaven . . ."

"I want rain! And you will bring it!" Bullit bellowed, heading for the door. "You are the only one who can! Just remember—it's your choice. Either you'll be a rich man or you'll be out in the street."

Just a Question of Adjustment

All that night, in his quavering voice, Old Solem muttered prayers to heaven. And toward morning, it began to rain. But it was not water that fell from the sky . . . not water, which would have quenched the ground's thirst. No, it began to rain flowers.

Petals of roses, blossoms of mimosa, azaleas, and tulips . . . all of them flowers that had never grown on Yatag. The air was still stifling, even though now it was perfumed with the mingled fragrances of millions of blossoms. In less than an

hour, the entire island was covered with a thick, many-colored carpet. People walked in petals up to their ankles. The children of Yatag loved it.

"Are you trying to make a fool of me, Solem?" Bullit tried hard to keep calm in the presence of the old man, but he felt ready to explode.

"When I put on the headdress of the ancient sorcerers of the Motecks, I never joke," Solem declared. "I must have made a tiny error in pronouncing the magic formula. It is just a question of an adjustment."

"Well," said Bullit, brushing an orchid from his hair. "It's true it has rained something. But my land and my herds need water, not flowers. Is that clear, you old madman?" Bullit thumped the television. "How would you watch this if I threw you out onto the street?"

"I'm tired," said the old man. "With everything that's happened, I haven't slept for two nights."

"Solem, your third attempt will be your last—and the one that had better succeed! You must succeed!"

Bullit took a wad of bills out of his shirt pocket. He put them on top of the TV. "You see that? There will be three times that amount for you if you can make it rain tomorrow. If not . . ."

Old Solem rose to his feet. "Most of the animals that graze on this island belong to you. You own more than

half the land . . . our houses . . . but you also want the sky, the sun, the clouds, everything . . ."

"That's right. I want everything . . . and more . . ."

Old Solem sighed. "It will rain tomorrow. Now get out and leave me in peace. It's time for my program."

There You Are . . . It's Done!

That night, so it is said, a cool breeze came in from the west and swept away the perfumed carpet of petals that had covered the island. Old Solem, wearing the garb of the Moteck sorcerers, studied the thick clouds that masked the moon and stars. He breathed deeply before continuing with the chant of his ancestors.

For a long time, his voice accompanied the moaning of the wind. The song he sang was halting, the steps he danced were clumsy, but he continued chanting and shuffling for more than an hour without leaving the circle of ash that he had laid out on the ground. Once in a while he paused, perhaps searching for the right words, or maybe to see the change that was taking place in the sky above him.

Old Solem was exhausted, but he kept going around and around in the circle, lifting his arms to the heavens,

until the first drops of water splashed down onto the ashes. Only then did his trembling legs stop their feeble dancing, did his ancient chant end with a sigh.

They were the first raindrops of what became a torrent. Accompanied by the loudest thunder and the brightest lightning the people of Yatag had ever heard and seen, the storm attacked the island. The deluge continued all through the night and into the next day.

Toward the end of the afternoon, Bullit arrived, his clothes dripping. He entered Old Solem's house without knocking.

"I knew you could do it! I have come to pay you what I promised," he shouted. Bullit advanced toward the armchair, waving a pudgy, money-stuffed hand in Solem's direction. "And now you must stop the storm. My crops don't need more water. Very soon it will be time to gather them in. I need fine, dry weather to bring in my harvest. Make it stop! Do you hear me? It has rained long enough! Get out there and make it stop. Now!"

He did not understand at first that Old Solem couldn't hear him. He seemed to be just dozing in his armchair, the TV control clutched in his wrinkled old hand. Then the reality became clear to Bullit. He felt the old man's cold fingers and knew that Old Solem was dead. He looked at the money in his hand and smiled. Stepping over to the TV, he picked up the bills he had left the day before. He looked around with satisfaction before going out the door.

The rain didn't stop. By the end of the first week, it was clear that the crops were ruined—a total loss. There would be no harvest that year.

Two months later, Bullit was still wondering when the terrible downpour would end.

Terror in the Night

Night! Darkness! A time of mystery and terror, monsters, ghosts, evil spirits . . . are they out there?

■ Dead People Walking

Did you ever see a *ghost◆*? A lot of people have, or think they have. Perhaps it is a white shape floating in a cemetery. Other ghosts are not seen, but heard. There are footsteps in abandoned houses, the sound of chains clanking or low moans in old castles . . . What do you think? Do the dead walk?

◆A ghost is the spirit of a dead person.

■ Hunters of the Night

Because it is quieter at night, sounds travel greater distances and seem more important. Footsteps that would scarcely be noticed during the day, may seem menacing after dark! There *are* real dangers in the night. Some of the great cats prefer to hunt by darkness. Even today, in jungle areas of India, many people each year are killed and eaten by tigers. Villagers tell tales of children pulled from their beds in the middle of the night, never to be seen again. Only a trail of blood and paw prints supply evidence of what happened.

■ Death by Moonlight

When the moon is full, do some people change? Do their teeth become fangs? Do they drop to all fours to hunt in the moonlight—no longer human? There is no real evidence for

werewolves, but the stories are still told. There are also tales of vampires and other weird beings that claim the night as their realm.

■ Monsters in Your Dreams

What's the scariest dream you've ever had? Was it of falling endlessly toward your death? Or perhaps of being all alone in empty nothing, screaming for help that never came? Nightmares take many shapes, but they can't really hurt you. Usually, just at the very moment when something terrible is about to happen, you find yourself awake—and safe—in your bed.

■ Cold Flames of Darkness

In a slimy bog or an old forest, the leaves of decades lie on the ground. Wander there by night and you might see cold "flames" dancing. Evil spirits? No, just the chemical glow (like that of fireflies) given off by a fungus that thrives on rotting organic material.

See a Ghos

Look steadily at the ghost below for 30 seconds, then shift your eyes to the castle gate. A pale "ghost" should appear.

What's Going On?

The "ghost" you have just seen is an example of an optical illusion called an *afterimage*. After you stared at the black ghost for awhile, the image remained on the retina at the back of your eye. When you shifted your vision to the white opening in the "castle gate," your brain "saw" an unaccustomed whiteness.

■ Tricking Your Senses

1. Look at the tiny squares within the larger ones. The inner colors of each pair are identical. But although they are exactly the same, the surrounding square (of black or white) makes them *appear* to be slightly different.

2. Stare at the intersections of the white lines between the small blue squares. You will see that spots of gray seem to appear at these points.

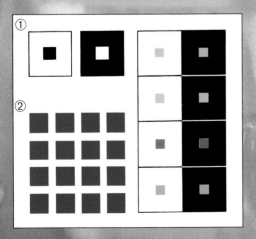

Amazing Mirages

Because of tricks of the mind and mirages, people see things that aren't really there.

■ Wishful Thinking

Scientists believe that tales of travelers who see green oases rising above the burning sands are best explained as tricks of the mind. These wishful *hallucinations* are not true mirages.

■ What Is a True Mirage?

True mirages are caused by the bending of light rays through air layers of different temperatures. Did you ever look down a paved road on a hot day and see a bright pool of water that you knew wasn't there? What you saw was a true mirage, a displaced image of the sky above.

■ Ships that Sail in the Air

A strange kind of true mirage is sometimes seen by sailors at sea. Looking at a distant ship, they may see it sailing in the air, not on water. This kind of displaced-image mirage happens because a cold layer of air lies next to the water surface, below a hotter layer. The bending of light rays moves the apparent image upward. You can't always believe what you see.

■ Mirages in the Heavens

In space, light beams can be bent when they pass close to star clusters. Some apparent pairs of stars may be one star seen twice!

The Monste

If you visited Loch❦ Ness in Scotland, might you see a strange creature rising from its depths?

■ An Old Legend

For more than 1,000 years, people living near Loch Ness in Scotland have reported sightings of a huge unknown creature in the lake. It is said that Nessie (as the supposed creature is familiarly dubbed) has devoured swimmers, upset fishermen's boats, and even come out of the water to terrify tourists and motorists on nearby roads!

❦Loch is a Scotch word meaning lake. Thus, Loch Ness means the Lake of Ness.

❦ Plesiosaur
A large, marine reptile that flourished millions of years ago.

■ Is There a Monster in the Lake?

If there is a creature in Loch Ness, what would it be? One of the most amazing theories suggested is that the creature is a *plesiosaur*❦, a fish-eating dinosaur, generally thought to be extinct.

n the Lake

True

The Search for Nessie

Thousands of people in modern times have reported strange sightings
in Loch Ness. Millions of dollars have been offered for proof of the creature's
existence. Scientists have searched the lake from end to end, but Nessie
has never been found.

Dark Waters of Mystery

Skeptics say that Nessie remains undiscovered because she
doesn't exist. But others point out that Loch Ness is 23 miles
(37 km) long, and extremely deep—a great place for a monster
to hide. The investigations continue.

The *Yeti* and *Bigfoot*

Do huge, hairy, man-like creatures inhabit the wild places of Earth?

Yeti
A supposed man-like creature of the frozen Himalayas.

Bigfoot
Creatures known as Bigfoot are reported to roam the mountainous and forested regions of the American Northwest.

Footprints in the Snow

In 1951, mountaineers searching for ways to scale Mount Everest found and photographed a trail of huge footprints in the high mountain snows. Were they evidence of the Yeti, a man-like creature believed by many to inhabit these lonely regions? To this day, the footprints have never been explained.

Shy Creatures of the American Wild

Over the years, campers and hikers have reported sightings of a huge, shy creature in remote parts of the West. In 1967, a Bigfoot may actually have been caught on film in the mountain forests of northern California. The 24 seconds of film show a tall, hairy, ape-like creature moving away into the trees. Expert analysis has not detected any evidence of fraud.

True

■ The Skeptics Confounded

As late as the nineteenth century, most scientists said that reports of a huge ape living undiscovered in the jungle mountains of Central Africa were sheer hokum. They were wrong. You have probably seen these mountain gorillas on television. They are very big . . . and very real!

■ All Over the World

Other man-like creatures are reported in many wild places—in frigid Siberia . . . the jungles of the South American Andes . . . the remote deserts of Asia. Natives insist that the "wild men" are real. In the face of so many reports, scientists must wonder—just as we do. To date, however, there are no explanations.

They Drink

"I hate garlic and love blood. I sleep all day and hunt at night. I am a corpse, but immortal. Who am I?"

■ A Savage Legend

Long ago, Count Dracula is said to have terrorized southeastern Europe. His ghoulish method of executing his enemies was to drive wooden stakes through their flesh. Historians believe that tales of this bloody count gave rise to the Legend of the Vampire.

■ The Modern Story

Many elements of the modern legend of the vampire were invented by a writer named Bram Stoker, in his 1897 novel *Dracula*. In this tale, an evil count lives in a gloomy castle in Transylvania. By drinking the blood of fresh victims, he lives forever. In recent years, many movies with vampire themes have added new details to our ideas about vampires.

Blood

■ Guarding Yourself Against Vampires

How do you recognize a vampire? Sharp teeth are one sign.
Also, a vampire makes no reflection in a mirror, and cannot
stand sunlight. A cross or garlic *may* drive him away.
How do you kill him? Easy. Just drive a wooden stake
through his heart!

■ There Are Real Vampires!

If you want to meet real vampires,
you should go to South America.
They aren't people, of course—
they're bats. Two species of
them usually feed on the
blood of cattle, but they
have been known
to attack humans.

Throughout history, people have believed that life on Earth is affected by the Moon.

■ Super Bleach?

People have always been fascinated by a full moon, believing it has powerful effects, not only on human beings, but on many earthly activities. A few generations back, women would wash white sheets and clothing at the time of a full moon, then spread the wet wash out on the grass overnight. They believed that the light of a full moon would bleach their linens to super whiteness.

Moonlight Magic

▮ Powerful Pull

The moon's gravity pulls at the water in Earth's oceans. High tides, low tides—we have them because of the moon. But do the hairs on your head and the carrots in your garden grow faster when the moon is full? Some people think so, but it is not true.

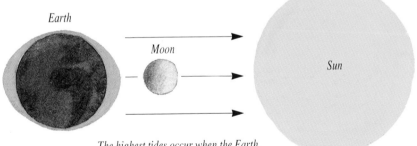

Earth

Moon

Sun

The highest tides occur when the Earth, the Moon, and the Sun are aligned.

▮ Moon Babies

The Romans believed that their moon goddess Diana controlled fertility and could grant pregnant women easy deliveries. Today, many people are convinced that women close to the time of delivery will give birth when the moon is full. However, research shows that there are no more births on these nights than on others.

Silence, We're Rolling!

Game

Pretty good, Mr. Director, but aren't there a few things wrong? See if you can find 22 mistakes on this movie set.

Answers on page 63.

It's Writter

For thousands of years, many people have believed that the stars determine our destinies.

■ Ancient Stargazers

Four thousand years ago, the Babylonians gazed in wonder at the night sky. They mapped the visible stars and noted the movements of the planets. Their studies were the beginning of *astrology*⛊ and *astronomy*⛊.

⛊ *Astrology tries to understand human destiny by linking it to patterns in the heavens.*

⛊ *Astronomy is the science of heavenly bodies.*

ן the Stars

The zodiac contains 12 signs used by astrologers to tell fortunes and predict the future.

■ What Is Your Sign?

The Babylonians divided the *zodiac* into 12 signs, named after groups of stars in the sky, which astronomers call constellations. The day you were born determines your astrological sign. These are the Twelve Astrological Signs and the days they govern: Aries, the Ram (March 21–April 19); Taurus, the Bull (April 20–May 20); Gemini, the Twins (May 21–June 21); Cancer, the Crab (June 22–July 22); Leo, the Lion (July 23–August 22); Virgo, the Virgin (August 23–September 22); Libra, the Scales (September 23–October 23); Scorpio, the Scorpion (October 24–November 21); Sagittarius, the Archer (November 22–December 21); Capricorn, the Goat (December 22–January 19); Aquarius, the Water-bearer (January 20–February 18); and Pisces, the Fish (February 19–March 20).

■ Believers and Skeptics

Those who believe in astrology think that the sign under which you were born tells a lot about what kind of person you are and what will happen in your life. Unbelievers say that the stars have little to do with human affairs. What do you think?

The Powe

■ Telepathy

Did you ever know exactly what someone was going to say before he or she said it? We call this kind of "mind reading" *telepathy*. Science explains these events as sheer coincidence. The people who have experienced them are not so sure.

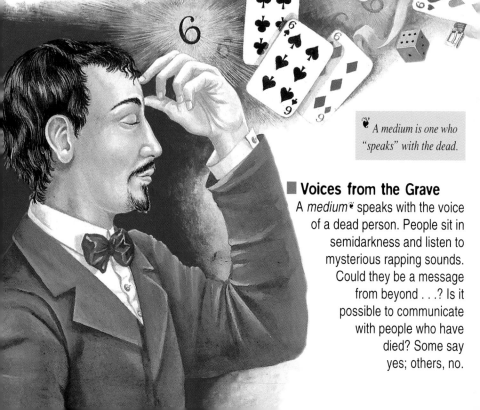

❦ *A medium is one who "speaks" with the dead.*

■ Voices from the Grave

A *medium*❦ speaks with the voice of a dead person. People sit in semidarkness and listen to mysterious rapping sounds. Could they be a message from beyond . . .? Is it possible to communicate with people who have died? Some say yes; others, no.

# of ESP

Clairvoyance

In 1759, a Swedish scientist, Emanuel Swedenborg, who was 300 miles (480 km) from Stockholm,

False

Sweden, suddenly cried out that he could "see" the city on fire. Many witnesses swore that he described the fire as it was burning. However, skeptics claimed that he told about his strange experience only long after the fire had happened. The Swedenborg story remains one of the most baffling incidences of claimed *clairvoyance* (psychic "seeing" at a distance).

Psychokinesis is the production of movement by psychic power.

Psychokinesis

The famed Israeli stage performer, Uri Geller, carried out many demonstrations in which spoons, untouched by hands or any other visible object, were made to bend. Geller's claim was that this could be explained by nothing other than *psychokinesis*. Professional magicians set out to prove Geller's claims false. With their tricks they were also able, it seemed, to bend spoons and other tableware. Can sheer mind power bend metal objects? Some people still believe that Geller used psychokinesis, but scientists disagree.

The Mysterious

Can a forked stick locate underground water or other treasures in the Earth?

■ A Long History

For centuries, miners of central Europe have practiced *dowsing* to locate minerals underground. Nobody knows exactly how, but dowsing works! Many mines discovered by dowsers are still in operation today.

■ Finding Water by Dowsing

Dowsing is using a divining rod to find underground water or minerals.

The *water-witch* walks slowly over the ground, holding the two slim forks of a divining rod. For a long time, perhaps, nothing happens. But suddenly the rod, seemingly of its own accord, points down. "Dig here!" the dowser says. "Here there is water." Astonishingly, water is frequently found at the indicated spot.

■ Dowsers for Hire

That dowsers can find water and locate other underground treasures such as oil and mineral deposits is sworn to by many thousands of satisfied customers. They include government agencies and multinational corporations who pay good money for dowsers' services. How does it work?

Water-witch is a popular term for a dowser who seeks water.

)ivining Rod

■ Some Explanations

How do dowsers do it? Some scientists speculate that the human body somehow responds to electromagnetic fields surrounding water or deposits of metal ore in the earth. Others claim that dowsers use some kind of extrasensory power. Many dowsers believe that their success is the result of some magic power in the divining rod, but scientists have proved this belief to be a false one. There's no magic in the rod itself, since, for some dowsers, even an ordinary wire coat hanger seems to work as well as a forked stick.

The Mysteries

What kind of marvels might you see in the wondrous land of India?

■ The Dancing Snakes

A snake charmer on the crowded streets of Bombay plays a wailing tune. A giant cobra sways back and forth. Is the snake dancing to the music? Not really. Snakes are nearly deaf. What then? Scientists say that the cobra follows the motion, not the sound of the flute. The charmer moves in time to the music, and the snake follows along.

■ Amazing Persistence

For religious reasons, some Indian holy men perform amazing feats to conquer the needs of human flesh. Many have remained seated for years without moving, have stood so long with one arm raised that they cannot bring it down, or have traversed their giant country by rolling on the ground.

# of India

False

■ The "Bed of Nails"

Demonstrating that they have become insensitive to pain, practitioners of *yoga*, the Indian art of bodily control, may sit or lie on a bed of nails. The nails *do* penetrate the flesh, but no bleeding occurs. It's a case of mind over matter.

■ The Famous Indian Rope Trick

The Indian illusionist tells a rope lying coiled in a basket to rise into the air. As spectators gape, the rope rises. An assistant climbs the rope. How? One way this famous trick is possible is for the performer to have a hidden accomplice in a hole in the ground. The accomplice pushes up a rigid pole that only looks like a rope! A second accomplice then has no difficulty getting to the top of the pole.

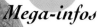

The Easter

The stone heads of Easter Island, some as much as 40 feet (12 m) tall, stand in eerie silence.

■ The Stone Giants

Along the shores of Easter Island, a lonely volcanic speck in the vastness of the Pacific, stand hundreds of huge stone heads carved from lava. In some areas of the island, rows of heads peer out at the ocean. How could the primitive people of Easter Island carve and move these monstrous statues, which weigh as much as 90 tons?

■ Strange Theories

Puzzled, theorists have proposed some strange explanations: the statue makers were really extraterrestrials . . . the stones were floated through the air by priests with magic powers . . . the Easter Islanders are descendants of an ancient advanced civilization that used methods and energies unknown to us today.

sland Puzzle

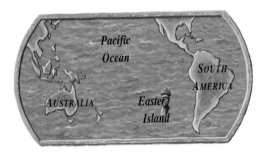

Pacific Ocean

SOUTH AMERICA

AUSTRALIA

Easter Island

The Archaeological Evidence

But it now seems likely, as Easter Islanders themselves believe, that their ancestors erected the statues at a time when the island's population was much greater. Using many men, hauling the stones with ropes, the statues were stood on end and "walked" to their final resting places.

Why Did They Do It?

To explain the why of the statues, anthropologists look to Polynesian societies, in which ancestor worship is common. Most probably the great stone statues are ancestral sentinels, guarding the people and their land from danger.

Ancient Astronauts,

Strange drawings on the Plains of Nazca baffle investigators.

■ Huge Drawings

They are the largest pictures ever made by humans. They lie open to view on the treeless plains of the Peruvian desert, yet they were not discovered until 1941. Only then did aviators flying over these desolate regions report that huge sections of the desert were covered with strange pictures and designs—giant birds, geometrical patterns, spirals, and swirls.

or . . . ?

True

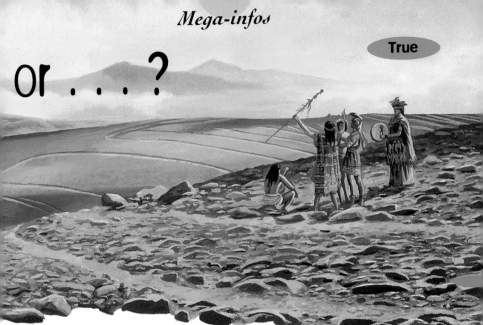

The Land of No Rain

There has been no significant rainfall on the Plains of Nazca for thousands of years. Only this lack of rain has preserved the designs, which were made by moving away the topmost layer of reddish pebbles, exposing the bare dirt below. The lack of rain also prevented the growth of plants, which would have destroyed the pictures.

Who Made These Strange Designs?

Investigators of the Nazca designs were puzzled by one intriguing fact—they cannot be seen as pictures from the ground. Some people think this must mean that they were made by ancient astronauts! More probable is that people of long ago made them for religious reasons. *Archaeologists* have even discovered scale models scratched on stone. The designs were probably then laid out on the ground with stakes and string. Once the strings were in place, the ancient Peruvians could remove the layer of pebbles, creating the huge images that they would never be able to view.

Archaeologists
People who study the remains of ancient civilizations.

39

Suddenly You See

**At a certain angle, a strange
scribble suddenly makes
sense!**

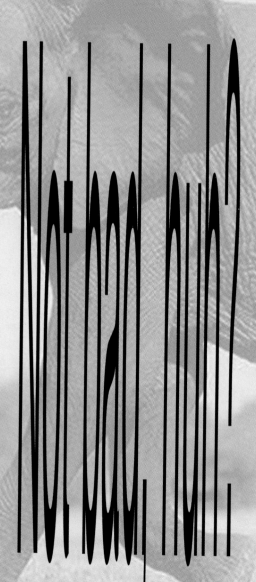

Secret Messages
To read this message,
tilt the book and close an
eye! To communicate
with your friends, nothing
is better than secret
messages. The code?
Write extremely elongated
letters.

■ Create a Distorted Image

1. Draw a grid for a normal drawing.

2. Draw a second grid and copy your drawing. To see the drawing more normally, tilt the paper and hold it a little ways away from your eye.

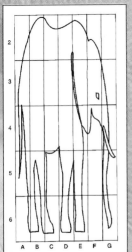

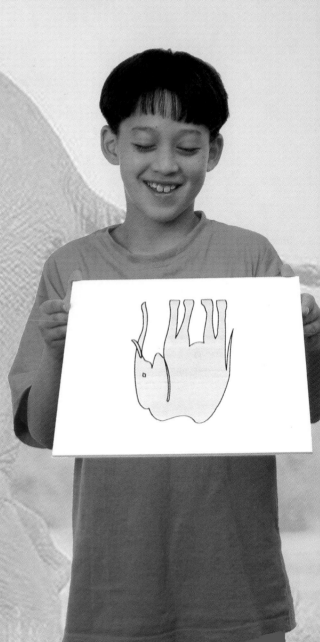

Megaliths

How did ancient people move the megaliths, the huge stones with which they built the thousands of monuments that dot western Europe?

❦ *Druids are the priests of certain prehistoric tribes.*

■ The Mystery of Stonehenge

Stonehenge, a giant circle of stones in southern England, may have been an astronomical observatory. Or was it a monument to the dead? Or a religious shrine? Some think that the *druids*❦ used the mysterious rocks as a site for human sacrifice.

■ Who Built Stonehenge?

The druids may have used Stonehenge, but they could not have begun its construction. Work on Stonehenge may have started more than 5,000 years ago, long before the druids and their tribes ever came to England from other parts of Europe.

■ Dolmens and Standing Stones

More than 50,000 mysterious stone structures have been found scattered across western Europe. Some of these are long lines of standing stones. Others, called *dolmens,* consist of two or more upright stones supporting a third lying across the top.
Excavations have turned up bones, weapons, and jewelry at dolmen sites. Some legends tell of fairies dancing beneath the massive arches.

■ How Were the Monuments Built?

Some of the stones at Stonehenge came from a site more than 200 miles (320 km) away. How did primitive people move them so far? How did they stand them upright? How did they raise huge stones atop others? We don't know all the answers, but it is believed that the giant stone monuments of Europe were transported and put in place by human muscle power alone!

Stonehenge means "hanging stones".

The Pharaoh's

After thousands of years, did the buried king punish the archaeologists who robbed his tomb?

■ The Tomb of Tutankhamen

February 1923 . . . Howard Carter and his team penetrate the tomb of the pharaoh Tutankhamen (King "Tut"), who ruled Egypt more than 3,000 years earlier. They find treasures beyond imagination. They tell of inscriptions that threaten death to any who violate the royal grave. In the next two years, 24 workers who entered the tomb died mysteriously. Did they fall victims to the curse?

■ The Mystery

Many of the archaeologists and workmen who died suffered from a strange congestion of the lungs, a malady doctors were unable to treat. What could the disease have been? A possible answer was discovered in 1957, when an illness known as "cave sickness" was identified. Bats often live in underground passages. A microscopic fungus grows in their droppings. This fungus can be deadly to those who breathe it! It seems quite possible that this rare disease may have been the cause of the strange illnesses and mysterious deaths.

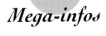

False

Curse

■ The Curse Was a Hoax

In 1980, a survivor of the Carter expedition revealed that the curse had been a hoax. It was invented by the archaeologists themselves to keep thieves away from the dig during the seven years of careful excavation. If it was a hoax, it was successful. All of the treasures were removed safely. But many still insist that King Tut reached beyond the grave to strike down those who disturbed his tomb.

Curious

SAVE THAT FIZZ!

Champagne is a kind of wine with bubbles of carbon dioxide fizz in it. Once opened, the bubbles escape, and in a short time the champagne goes flat. Champagne connoisseurs once believed that the handle of a spoon stuck in the neck of a bottle would hold in the bubbles. Tests proved that this doesn't work.

SWIRLING IN THE DRAIN

Pull the plug from a sink or washbasin, and the water will swirl as it goes down the drain. Amazingly, the swirl always goes in the same direction—clockwise in the Northern Hemisphere, counterclockwise in the Southern. Why? It's because of the rotation of the Earth, which pulls at the gurgling liquid.

ut True!

● PHOTOGRAPHS OF FAIRIES

Have fairies, the mythical spirits of the European forest, been captured on film? Early in the twentieth century, two English children astounded their family and friends with photographs showing quaint fairy-like creatures. Decades later, they admitted that the photographs were made by hanging painted cardboard outlines on branches.

IT'S RAINING FROGS!

Frogs do rain from the sky! How can this be? Are there celestial frogs swimming and croaking in the clouds? Of course not. But frogs can fall from the sky if a tornado or whirlwind snatches them up and later drops them.

The Lost Continent

A rich and prosperous civilization . . . divine punishment . . . a continent that sank beneath the sea . . . Atlantis♥!

■ A Legend Begins

Plato, the Greek philosopher, died more than 2,000 years ago. Yet, a story he told still leads people on a search for the lost continent of Atlantis. Many believe it was destroyed by an earthquake, followed by a tidal wave.

♥ Atlantis, according to the legend, is a huge island in the Atlantic Ocean

■ It's Here, It's There, It's Anywhere . . .

Thousands of books and articles have been written about Atlantis. It is described as a paradise on Earth, governed by wise men. Evidence "proves" that it was in the Mediterranean . . . beyond *Gibraltar* 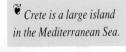 . . . in the Caribbean . . . in the Pacific . . . in the North Sea . . .

❦ Gibraltar is the narrow strait between Europe and Africa. To the west lies the Atlantic Ocean; to the east, the Mediterranean Sea.

❦ Crete is a large island in the Mediterranean Sea.

■ The Earthquake that Destroyed Santorini

Santorini is a small island near *Crete* in the eastern Mediterranean. Geologists have determined that a monster earthquake destroyed Santorini about 1400 B.C. Crete is not far from Athens, the city in Greece where Plato lived and taught. Is the myth of Atlantis an old memory of this ancient disaster?

■ The Search Continues

What are the strange stone structures in the Caribbean, off the Bimini Islands? Some say that they are natural formations, but others believe that they are the ruins of Atlantis. Or did Plato simply make up the story to prove a point about how governments should be run? Will we ever know?

The Seas of Death

Florida, Bermuda, and Puerto Rico bound a triangle of more than 400,000 square miles (1,000,000 km^2) of the Atlantic Ocean. Is the area cursed?

■ **Many Ships and Planes Have Vanished**

Many ships have sunk under strange circumstances in the deadly Bermuda Triangle. In 1914, the ship *Cyclops*, with 309 people aboard, disappeared in a calm sea. Though the *Cyclops* had a radio, no distress signal was ever received. In 1976, the tanker *Grand Zenith* went down with all hands. In 1945, a training flight of five torpedo bombers mysteriously disappeared over these waters. And so did the plane that went to search for them!

Additional Mysteries

Accidents at sea are not uncommon. Storms, icebergs, collisions—these happen everywhere; however, the absence of distress calls in so many of the disappearances is unusual. The fact that survivors are seldom found has also added to the mystery of the Bermuda Triangle.

Maybe There's No Mystery At All

Scientific analysis of Bermuda Triangle ship and plane wrecks seems to show that the number of disasters in these waters is not really surprising. They are, after all, among the most heavily traveled sea lanes on Earth.

Columbus Started the Story

Some students of history think that Christopher Columbus was first responsible for the gloomy reputation of the Bermuda Triangle. On his first voyage to the New World, lack of wind stranded his ships there for days. The sailors were bothered by huge patches of floating seaweed. Upset by this dismal experience, they advised others to avoid the area. Perhaps this was the beginning of the area's long history of misfortunes that continues to this day.

Don't You

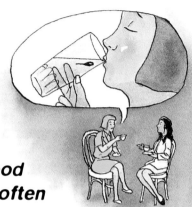

People like a good story. They will often repeat an exciting rumor whether they believe it or not.

■ Stories Grow

Alligators have been found alive in the sewers of New York! That's true. Perhaps they were little ones purchased as pets. But as the story is told, the alligators get bigger and bigger. After awhile, tales are told of monster man-eaters beneath the sidewalks!

■ Can You Believe What You Read?

"BODIES OF SPACE ALIENS FOUND IN MONTANA!" You see the headline screaming from a tabloid newspaper. Can you believe it? Well . . . of course many of these stories are entirely made up.

Believe It!

■ Good Stories, but Very Tall Tales

. . . A woman swallowed a tadpole. Later, during an operation, a giant frog jumped from her belly . . . A driver picks up a young girl hitchhiking. She rides with him for awhile, but at a certain bend of the road, POOF!—she disappears. He goes to the police station and is informed that some time ago, at that same place on the road, a young girl was killed in an accident. Stories like these are told and retold. Some even appear in print. But you can't believe everything you hear or read!

■ Seeing Is Believing, or Is It?

A photograph or a video clip shows flying saucers in the sky. Can you believe everything you see? Probably not. Many frauds have been discovered, and more will no doubt be attempted.

Unidentified Flying Object

Is our planet being observed by aliens?
Do they spy on us from their UFOs?

Flying saucers is the term used for UFOs of many shapes.

■ The First Flying Saucers

"They flew like a saucer that you skipped across water." So reported Kenneth Arnold, the American businessman who said he saw a flight of strange silent aircraft in 1947. The press coined the term *"flying saucers"* ❦. Soon, thousands of other sightings, all over the world, were being reported. In fact, new sightings are still being reported—almost on a daily basis.

■ Alarm in the U.S. Air Force

What if the flying saucer UFOs were machines operated by enemy forces . . . or by beings from another planet? The Air Force, naturally concerned, began Project Bluebook. They studied 12,618 UFO sightings. They explained away most of them, but were forced to classify 701 as "unexplained."

■ Are They Real?

Tales of UFOs remain one of the great unsolved mysteries of our times. They've been seen by airplane pilots and astronauts, as well as from the ground. They've been watched on radar, captured in photographs. Theories multiply.

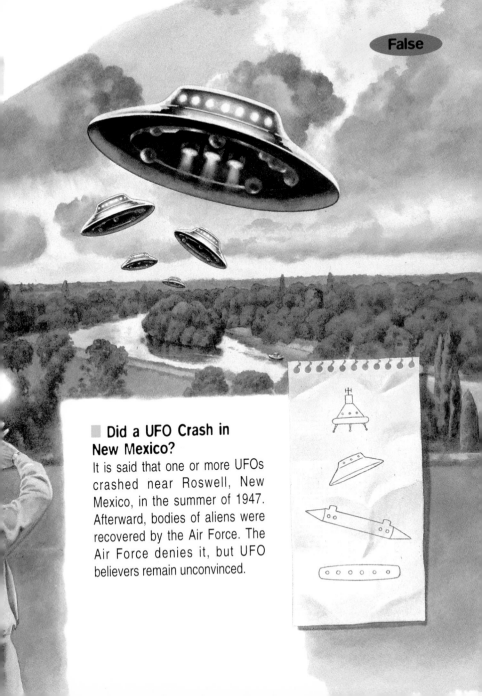

■ Did a UFO Crash in New Mexico?

It is said that one or more UFOs crashed near Roswell, New Mexico, in the summer of 1947. Afterward, bodies of aliens were recovered by the Air Force. The Air Force denies it, but UFO believers remain unconvinced.

E.T.s—Are They Here?

Are they watching us?
Do they kidnap people?
Have they already taken over
our world and we don't know it?

■ Tales of the Aliens

You've seen extraterrestrials (E.T.s) in the movies. They have been shown as invaders that come to wage war on our planet. They've also been creatures of peace, bringing wisdom and healing to our troubled world. Sometimes they look just like us. Sometimes they are many-armed monsters seeking human flesh to devour.

■ Abductions by Aliens?

Many people believe that they have been kidnapped by aliens while driving down lonely roads, or even right from their beds at home. Often they claim to have been transported inside UFOs where they are medically examined by strange humanoid creatures. Sometimes the aliens are silent; sometimes they speak. Some people report having been repeatedly abducted. Such stories are disturbing. What do you think?

True

Will Humans Someday Be Aliens?

As mankind takes the first steps into space, we can ask: At some time in the future, will we land on far planets where *we* will be the extraterrestrials?

■ Myths are ancient religions.

False. Myths are ancient *stories*. They may or may not be religious in nature.

■ You can see mirages in the Gobi Desert.

False. The Gobi is a cold desert. Mirages are seen in hot deserts.

■ People were really burned as witches.

True. In the Middle Ages in Europe, thousands of people found guilty of witchcraft were executed, many by burning.

■ Some metals bend and unbend when heated.

True. Alloys have been created that, after having been bent, will return to their original shape when reheated.

alse?

The ancients ad techniques or moving huge locks of stone.

Plants have feelings.

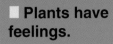

Maybe. Some scientific experiments seem to show that plants respond to human emotions.

Astrologers can predict the future.

There is life on Mars.

True. The ancients had only their own strength and simple tools. By working together, however, they were able to transport enormous stones over great distances.

False. However, if enough predictions are made, some of them are bound to come true.

True. Signs of life on the cellular level have recently been discovered.

■ Fake medicines can heal.

True. Doctors call this the *placebo effect*. People given fake pills or injections can experience relief from their symptoms. It's an example of the power of mind over matter.

■ Scientists are not interested in imaginary animals.

False. *Cryptozoologists* are scientists who think that a make-believe animal may sometimes be confused with one that is real. This is how giant squid were discovered.

■ The mystery of the disappearing dinosaurs has been solved.

Maybe. Some researchers find strong evidence that a giant meteorite hit Earth 65 million years ago, wiping out the dinosaurs. Others suggest different explanations.

■ Miracle cures really happen.

True. No one is sure exactly how or why, but people who can't move their legs have suddenly walked. People with "incurable" cancers have recovered completely.

alse?

■ Underground minerals can be found with airplanes.

True. Sensitive instruments mounted in airplanes can "map" underground deposits, providing valuable clues to those in search of mineral riches.

■ Science and religion can never agree.

False. Many scientists believe in God; many people of all religions believe in science.

■ The Seven Ancient Wonders of the World have all been destroyed.

False. The ancient Wonders of the World were marvels—the hanging gardens of Babylon, great temples, tombs. Most have been destroyed by time, war, or earthquakes. But one remains—the Great Pyramids of Egypt.

■ Ancient Romans moved rocks that weighed an incredible 800 tons.

True. It must have taken hundreds or thousands of slaves to do it, but it is estimated that three of the stones at the Temple of Baalbek in Lebanon weigh that much. The stones are more than 65 feet (20 m) long, 13 feet (4 m) wide, and 13 feet (4 m) thick.

Index

Answers to the puzzle on pages 26–27.

You should have found: Make-up artist's feather duster; two moons; a backward witch's broom; camera facing wrong direction; director's megaphone not plugged in; carrot at end of soundman's boom; sound engineer's stethoscope; sound box not connected; man stabbed with sword; woman with backward torso; carnivorous plant eating telephone; painting of vampire with cross on its neck; ghost in patterned shroud; man with no head; dog with two heads; man walking up wall; portrait with no face; owl with a pig in its claws; torch held up by a foot; escalator; suit of armor with astronaut's helmet; man walking through solid wall.

Photo credits for stickers
The Kobal Collection; The Charles Walker Collection/Images Colour Library; AKG Photo London;
The Charles Walker Collection/Images Colour Library; Christophe Collection;
René Dahinden/Fortean Picture Library; The Charles Walker Collection/Images Colour Library.

Photo credits for picture cards (left to right)
p. 40-41: © Minden Pictures
Top: The Kobal Collection; The Charles Walker Collection/Images Colour Library; The Kobal Collection;
The Charles Walker Collection/Images Colour Library
Bottom: The Charles Walker Collection/Images Colour Library; René Dahinden/Fortean Picture Library;
René Dahinden/Fortean Picture Library; Griffith Institute/Ashmolean Museum Oxford; Tintin courtesy of
Moulinsart SA. Brussels; The Charles Walker Collection/Images Colour Library.

Illustrations
Ian Chamberlain, Izhar Cohen, Elaine Cox, Mark Edwards, Jeff Fisher, Daniel Guerrier, Michael Johnson,
Louise Kelly, Olivier Lemoine, Robert Mason, Danuta Mayer, Tony McSweeney, Caroline Thomson, Andrew Wheatcroft
Cover: Donald Grant

Stickers

The Kiss of the Vampire
(I. Adjani and K. Kinski, 1978).

The ghost in the movie *Ghostbusters*
had very bad manners.

If you glimpse the
primrose fairy at dawn,
she will bring you
good luck.

A holy man of India lying on a bed of nails.

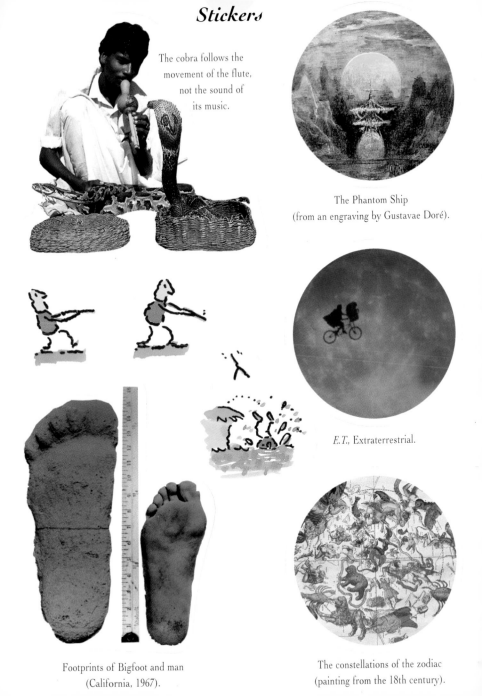

Stickers

The cobra follows the movement of the flute, not the sound of its music.

The Phantom Ship (from an engraving by Gustavae Doré).

E.T., Extraterrestrial.

Footprints of Bigfoot and man (California, 1967).

The constellations of the zodiac (painting from the 18th century).

King Kong

In the movie, King Kong is captured in Africa and taken to New York. There he has various adventures and eventually takes refuge on top of the Empire State Building. King Kong is depicted as having tender, human-like feelings, but he was not a hominid. He was a fictional, super-sized gorilla.

E. B. Shoedsack and M. Cooper, USA, 1933.

Easter Island Statues

These huge stone statues, which stand facing the sea on Easter Island in the Pacific Ocean, are one of the world's great mysteries. Who carved them? How were they moved? What was their purpose? Even the descendants of the original Easter Islanders don't know the answers.

Casper

Casper's a friendly ghost,
and an imaginary one. But
are there real ghosts? Are
the spirits of the dead able
to come back and haunt us?
What would you do if you
saw a ghost?

Silberling, USA, 1995.

The Cottingley Fairies

Taken in England in 1917,
this photograph shows a
ten-year-old girl with a
dancing fairy. At the time,
many people thought the
picture proved the existence
of fairies. Later, it was
discovered the photo was a hoax,
made with a cut-out fairy figure.

Bigfoot

There are still unexplored
places on our planet, but the
American Northwest is not
one of them. Yet rumors persist
that a manlike, apelike
· creature lives in the forests.
A 24-second strip of movie
film even seems to show one.

Nessie

In 1982, a photographer
caught this image of what
he claimed was the monster
that is reported to live in
Loch Ness, in Scotland.
But is the little blotch really
Nessie? Might it be a piece
of debris, or just a flaw
in the film?

The Megaliths of Stonehenge

The building of Stonehenge, in southern England, may have
begun more than 5,000 years ago. How were the giant rocks
hauled to the site and put in place? And why? Was Stonehenge
an astronomical observatory? A religious temple?
Will we ever know?

Salisbury Plain, England

King Tut's Tomb

The fabulous treasure of Tutankhamen's tomb was discovered
in 1923 in Egypt's Valley of the Kings. The tomb contained
statues, masks, jewels, ceremonial objects, and even food to
accompany the pharaoh on his journey to the life beyond
death. The deaths that occurred after the opening of the tomb
led people to believe there was a curse on any who entered it.

The Nazca Drawings

Only in 1941 were these mysterious drawings discovered on the Plains of Nazca, in Peru. Giant birds, insects, spirals, and other patterns so large that only from the air can they be recognized as having been made by humans. But who? When? Why?

Flying Saucers

Clouds, weather balloons, airplane lights, satellites . . . they all have been used to explain sightings of "flying saucers." But many people believe they are really visitors from another planet, or even from another dimension.

Camarillo, California

Diviners

Today's diviners, more commonly called dowsers, practice their mysterious art just as the diviners of the Middle Ages did, by using a forked stick to find water or minerals.

The Yeti

Is he real, the huge, hairy, manlike creature of the Himalayas? Mountain climbers claim they have seen his footsteps in the snow. Some say they have even caught sight of him.

TinTin in Tibet. Barron's, 1995.